Instant Apple iBooks How-to

Learn how to read and write books for iBookstore, by fully utilizing Apple iBooks and iBooks Author

Zeeshan Chawdhary

PUBLISHING

BIRMINGHAM - MUMBAI

Instant Apple iBooks How-to

First published: February 2013

Production Reference: 1180213

Published by Packt Publishing Ltd.
Livery Place
35 Livery Street
Birmingham B3 2PB, UK.

ISBN 978-1-84969-402-5

www.packtpub.com

Credits

Author
Zeeshan Chawdhary

Reviewer
Allen Sherrod

Acquisition Editor
Joanne Fitzpatrick

Commissioning Editor
Meeta Rajani

Technical Editor
Dennis John

Project Coordinator
Joel Goveya

Proofreader
Maria Gould

Graphics
Conidon Miranda

Shantanu Zagade

Production Coordinators
Conidon Miranda

Shantanu Zagade

Cover Work
Conidon Miranda

Cover Image
Valentina D'silva

About the Author

Zeeshan Chawdhary has over 8 years of experience in the web, mobile, and location-based services space. With a career spanning from 3D Mobile Game development at IndiaGames to leading a location-based travel startup at iCityConcierge Ltd. As the Chief Technology Officer, Zeeshan has been able to work on a lot of exciting technologies with a the focus on cutting-edge travel technologies.

Among his key achievements, he has pioneered in the right mix of using open source and proprietary software to create a technology stack based on the client's need. He has developed location-based solutions for Nokia (getting millions of hits per year) on a scalable cloud platform using Rackspace Cloud.

He enjoys working with PHP, PostGIS, and PhoneGap. He has immense experience in creating startups that use location data effectively for their growth; from startups for companies such as Foursquare to hotel industry big-wigs like Marriott; from mobile giant Nokia to airline king American Airlines, he has worked with them all.

Zeeshan currently serves as the CTO of iCityConcierge Ltd, where he is currently working on creating the best personalized travel experience for travellers. He can be reached on Google at `imzeeshanc@gmail.com`.

Firstly, I am grateful to God for he made me what I am. I would like to thank my parents who have always been supportive for my love of books and computers. I would also like to thank my wife Sundus, who has been a great support while I wrote this book in the wee hours. I also thank my brother and sister for enduring me all these years.

About the Reviewer

Allen Sherrod is currently a senior iOS developer of interactive apps with several apps in the iTunes store which includes DreamWorks movies such as *Rise of the Guardians*, and the upcoming film, *The Croods*. Allen started with programming in high school as he learned OpenGL and Direct3D for the first time. From there he took to game development as a hobby throughout college, wrote several books on the topic, and now he currently creates interactive storybook and comic apps for mobile platforms.

He has also authored and co-authored several books such as *Essential XNA Game Studio 2.0 Programming, Jones & Bartlett Publishers*; *Data Structures and Algorithms for Game Developers, Charles River Media*; and *Beginning DirectX 11 Game Programming, Course Technology PTR*, to name a few.

> I would like to thank my family and friends for always supporting and helping me over the years through both good and bad times.

www.packtpub.com

Support files, eBooks, discount offers and more

You might want to visit www.packtpub.com for support files and downloads related to your book.

Did you know that Packt offers eBook versions of every book published, with PDF and ePub files available? You can upgrade to the eBook version at www.packtpub.com and as a print book customer, you are entitled to a discount on the eBook copy. Get in touch with us at service@packtpub.com for more details.

At www.packtpub.com, you can also read a collection of free technical articles, sign up for a range of free newsletters and receive exclusive discounts and offers on Packt books and eBooks.

http://packtlib.packtpub.com

Do you need instant solutions to your IT questions? PacktLib is Packt's online digital book library. Here, you can access, read and search across Packt's entire library of books.

Why Subscribe?

- ▶ Fully searchable across every book published by Packt
- ▶ Copy and paste, print and bookmark content
- ▶ On demand and accessible via web browser

Free Access for Packt account holders

If you have an account with Packt at www.packtpub.com, you can use this to access PacktLib today and view nine entirely free books. Simply use your login credentials for immediate access.

Table of Contents

Preface

iBooks is an amazing application from Apple that makes a great reading experience for book lovers. All your books, be they PDF, EPUB, or Apple iBook format, can now be organized directly within iBooks. iBooks provides an intuitive way to organize, read, and annotate your book content. You as a reader have so many options to explore within iBooks; you can read, buy, and share what you are reading with your friends.

If you are too lazy to read, you can even listen to the book using Apple VoiceOver on your iPad. Synching your book collection across various iOS devices is now a breeze, and with support for iCloud, all your books can be available to all your iOS devices, all the time!

The Apple iBookstore that is neatly integrated in the iBooks application allows the user to buy free and paid books from thousands of authors worldwide, immediately—you don't have to wait for the shipment to arrive any longer!

With iBooks Author, Apple has also allowed publishers to create compelling storybooks, textbooks that not only include text, but also animations, graphics, 3D content, and music. In fact there are many books out there that have minima; text and more multimedia.

What this book covers

Downloading iBooks from the iTunes store (Must know) will get you started with iBooks by downloading the iBooks app on your iOS devices.

Browsing and shopping for books in the iBookstore (Should know) will teach you how to browse and shop for books in the iBookstore via the iBooks app.

Using reading tools (Should know) explains tagging, annotating, and sharing what you are reading with your social networks.

Making and managing Collections (Should know) explains the concept of the collections and shows you how to create one and add books to it.

Adding PDFs to the iBooks Library (Should know) explains importing PDFs from various sources (e-mail, web, other apps) into iBooks.

Publishing your own books with iBooks Author (Should know) explains the use of the iBooks Author tool to create a book, and explains its features.

Exploring iBooks Author templates (Should know) explains the various templates available with iBooks Author that allows for the faster creation of a book's layout.

Building a London travel guide with iBooks Author (Become an expert) takes you on a journey to write a full Apple iBooks-supported London travel guide book using iBooks Author by utilizing the great encyclopedia of our modern times, `www.Wikipedia.org`, as well as `www.WikiTravel.org`.

Adding HTML widgets and 3D models to your books (Become an expert) makes your book interactive by showing you how to integrate HTML widgets in your books as well as visualizing a 3D model from within a book page.

What you need for this book

To buy and read the books from iBookstore, you will need an iPad and the iBooks application from the iTunes store.

To write and test books using iBooks Author, you will need an Apple MacBook or iMac and the iBooks Author program from the Mac App Store.

Who this book is for

This book is for book lovers as well as publishers, writers, and authors who want to understand the Apple iBooks ecosystem.

This book will help book lovers to organize their book collection. For publishers, the book provides a good opportunity to try out the iBookstore model of publishing.

Conventions

In this book, you will find a number of styles of text that distinguish between different kinds of information. Here are some examples of these styles, and an explanation of their meaning.

New terms and **important words** are shown in bold. Words that you see on the screen, in menus or dialog boxes for example, appear in the text like this: "Open the iBooks App and hit the **Store** button on the top-left corner of the screen."

 Warnings or important notes appear in a box like this.

Tips and tricks appear like this.

Reader feedback

Feedback from our readers is always welcome. Let us know what you think about this book—what you liked or may have disliked. Reader feedback is important for us to develop titles that you really get the most out of.

To send us general feedback, simply send an e-mail to feedback@packtpub.com, and mention the book title via the subject of your message.

If there is a book that you need and would like to see us publish, please send us a note in the **SUGGEST A TITLE** form on www.packtpub.com or e-mail suggest@packtpub.com.

If there is a topic that you have expertise in and you are interested in either writing or contributing to a book, see our author guide on www.packtpub.com/authors.

Customer support

Now that you are the proud owner of a Packt book, we have a number of things to help you to get the most from your purchase.

Downloading the example code

You can download the example code files for all Packt books you have purchased from your account at http://www.packtpub.com. If you purchased this book elsewhere, you can visit http://www.packtpub.com/support and register to have the files e-mailed directly to you.

Errata

Although we have taken every care to ensure the accuracy of our content, mistakes do happen. If you find a mistake in one of our books—maybe a mistake in the text or the code—we would be grateful if you would report this to us. By doing so, you can save other readers from frustration and help us improve subsequent versions of this book. If you find any errata, please report them by visiting http://www.packtpub.com/support, selecting your book, clicking on the **errata submission form** link, and entering the details of your errata. Once your errata are verified, your submission will be accepted and the errata will be uploaded on our website, or added to any list of existing errata, under the Errata section of that title. Any existing errata can be viewed by selecting your title from http://www.packtpub.com/support.

Piracy

Piracy of copyright material on the Internet is an ongoing problem across all media. At Packt, we take the protection of our copyright and licenses very seriously. If you come across any illegal copies of our works, in any form, on the Internet, please provide us with the location address or website name immediately so that we can pursue a remedy.

Please contact us at `copyright@packtpub.com` with a link to the suspected pirated material.

We appreciate your help in protecting our authors, and our ability to bring you valuable content.

Questions

You can contact us at `questions@packtpub.com` if you are having a problem with any aspect of the book, and we will do our best to address it.

Instant Apple iBooks How-to

Welcome to *Instant Apple iBooks How-to*. This book will quickly teach you to work efficiently with iBooks on your iPad, organize and read books with iBooks, as well as teach you how to write your own book for iBooks using Apple's iBooks Author!

Downloading iBooks from the iTunes store (Must know)

The iBooks application is *not* pre-loaded on the iPhone and iPad, so users that want to read books on their iOS device need to download the iBooks app from iTunes.

Getting ready

To download and install apps from the iTunes store, you need to have an Apple ID registered and/or iTunes. An Apple ID is free to create, so don't hesitate to get one.

How to do it...

The iBooks App is available for download on `https://itunes.apple.com/us/app/ibooks/id364709193?mt=8` (current version being 3.0.2).

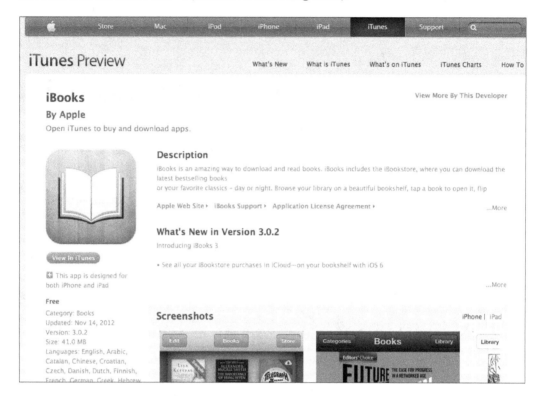

Visiting the mentioned link from your iOS device will open the iTunes App Store on your device. You can download the iBooks app like any other app. Alternately, users can also type in `iBooks` on their iPhone App Store to download the iBooks app.

The iBooks app is an application developed by Apple to work on iPhone, iPad, and iPod devices for e-book reading, annotation, Multi-Touch books, and textbooks. It supports the industry standard `.epub`, `.pdf`, and `.ibook` (Apple proprietary) formats for the books.

There's more...

The iBooks app also includes **iBookstore** that allows you to download e-books and textbooks available from various publishers.

Browsing and shopping books from the iBookstore (Should know)

iBookstore is an in-app store within the iBooks app that allows consumers to browse and download over 1.5 million books.

How to do it...

1. Open the iBooks App and hit the **Store** button on the top-left corner of the screen (on the iPad, on the iPhone it is on the top-right corner), to open the iBookstore, as shown in the following screenshot (iPad version):

2. You can switch back to your book library by tapping on the **Library** button on the top-left corner of the iBookstore window.

3. The iBookstore lists books by all categories by default. Various books on categories such as biography, fiction, history, travel, and adventure are available to download.

   Let us look at downloading a few books on London from the iBookstore. Open the iBookstore and search for **London**; you will get a plethora of books on London—from history of London to a book on London's underworld!

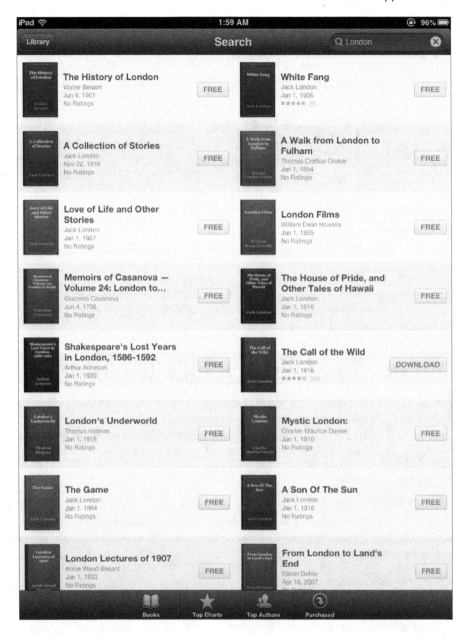

4. Tap on the **Free** button next to the book listings to download and add the book to your iBooks library.

5. Books can also be downloaded from the iTunes app on your Mac or Windows desktop. To do so, open iTunes and navigate to the iTunes store section, select **Books** from the navigation bar on the top.

There's more...

The books available via iBookstore vary from country to country. Some titles may not be available in your region.

Free and paid books are downloaded just as free and paid apps are downloaded for iPhone or iPad, from iTunes. If you have downloaded apps for your iOS devices via iTunes, you shouldn't have any problems downloading books as well.

Using reading tools (Should know)

iBooks allows us to select text, underline it, make a note on the selected text, search a word in the dictionary or the Internet, or even search within the book. Some interactive books can also play audio/video or even audio navigation using the read-aloud feature, for general books. The VoiceOver utility on your iOS device can read out a book to the user.

Getting ready

For VoiceOver, on your iPhone, navigate to **Settings | General | Accessibility** and slide **VoiceOver** to **On**. Remember that VoiceOver will change the iOS device's behavior depending on the following actions:

▶   Tapping once will select an item

▶   Double-tapping will activate the selected item

▶   Swiping three fingers will scroll the page

How to do it...

1. To copy, highlight, take a note, search, or share, double-tap the start of the text area and drag-select the required text; a pop up will appear on the page with the desired actions as seen in the following screenshot:

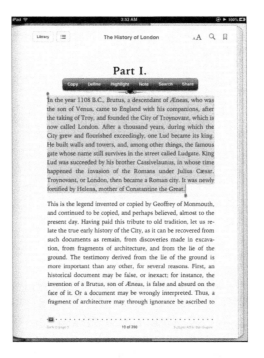

2. To highlight a text with different colors and underline it, just select the text with the highlighter and it will highlight the text (the default color is yellow).

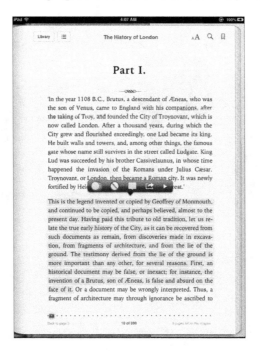

3. Tapping the highlighted text shows a pop-up menu to change to different colors or underline the text, as well as the option to remove the formatting completely.

4. Besides, the sharing option (e-mail, Facebook, Message, Twitter) becomes available with both, the regular double-tap-to-select-text and single-drag-to-select-text methods.

5. Another great feature for reading is **Fonts** and **Themes** that allows a reader to increase/decrease font size and font family, as well as change the background between white, sepia, and black—allowing for great customization of the reading experience.

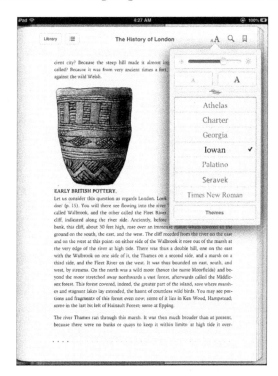

6. Here is the same page in night mode! Note that reading in night mode causes less strain to your eyes in the dark.

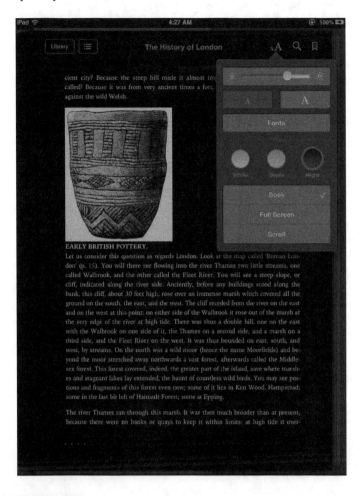

How it works...

iBooks has a great in-built functionality to make the reading experience as simple, elegant, and helpful as possible for a reader. No wonder sales of iBooks and iPads in the education sector are growing rapidly, so much so that some universities dole out iPads to students joining their courses.

There's more...

The in-built dictionary supports English, German, French, Spanish, Chinese, and Japanese.

Making and managing Collections (Should know)

If you are an avid reader of e-books and have hundreds of e-books and PDF files in your library, then you would know that managing, sorting, and organizing them in an efficient way is a tireless thing. With iBooks, you have an excellent way to organize and tag your books via **Collections**, something akin to creating folders and storing files therein.

We'll consider our previous example; we could download all books returned via the search for the keyword "London" and store them in a collection called "London" on our iOS device.

How to do it...

By default, iBooks has two collections: **Books** and **PDFs**, and as you buy books from the iBookstore, another collection gets added: **Purchased Books**.

1. Creating a collection:

    i. To store all books related to "London" that we downloaded from the iBookstore, we create a collection called London by tapping the **Collections** button on the iBooks app.

    ii. Then we'll tap on **New** to create a new collection and will name it London, as shown in the following screenshot:

2. Adding books to **Collections**:

    i.   Once we have downloaded the books and they are visible on the iBooks' bookshelf, we can add the books to a collection by tapping the **Edit** button on the top-right corner of the screen.

    ii.   Tap on the books we want to move to our collection and tap the **Move** option from the top-left corner of the screen and select **London** as shown in the following screenshot:

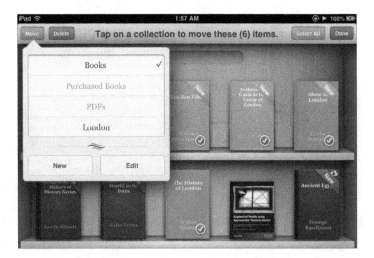

3. Moving, deleting, and re-arranging books in your collections:

    i.   Within our collection, we can move books to other collections as well as delete books by using the **Edit** button on the top-right corner within iBooks. You can re-arrange the books on the bookshelf by a simple drag-and-drop action.

ii. By default, the bookshelf displays books in a grid view, but we can change the view by selecting the List View icon on iBooks, which displays the books in a neat list that can be sorted by title, author, and category.

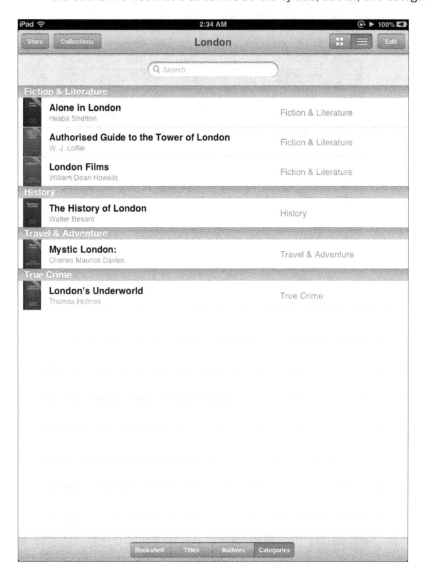

There's more...

If you have multiple iOS devices, you can sync the same iBooks experience of Collections on all your iOS devices, by setting the **Sync Collections** options in your device's **Settings** to **On**.

Adding PDFs to the iBooks library (Should know)

The most popular format for e-books is still PDF, since it makes a strong case for easy distribution and wide acceptance with multiple readers; desktop, web, and mobile all support PDF documents almost natively.

How to do it...

iOS devices detect PDF from e-mails, web pages, and so on and show an **Open in iBooks** button to open the PDF directly in iBooks.

I have some free PDF books from Packt Publishing ☺ in my account at `https://www.packtpub.com/`. I will download one of them and add it to iBooks via e-mail. Here is how a PDF can be added to iBooks from within an e-mail:

There's more...

PDFs can also be added to iBooks via iTunes and synced to your iPad or iPhone. The Sync option in iTunes provides an option to sync all the books or selected PDFs only.

Publishing your own books with iBooks Author (Should know)

Apple provides an excellent e-book publishing tool—**iBooks Author**, available free via the Mac App Store, a tool that makes writing interactive e-books for iPad a breeze.

The current Version 2.0 of iBooks Author supports the following features:

- ▶ Multi-Touch books
- ▶ Interactive images and video support
- ▶ 3D support
- ▶ Custom HTML widgets
- ▶ Export to PDF
- ▶ Custom fonts support
- ▶ Mathematical expressions support
- ▶ Retina display support
- ▶ Drag-and-drop content support
- ▶ Templates for common book formats—cookbooks, photo books, and so on
- ▶ Publishing books to iBookstore from within iBooks Author

 Note that the books produced by iBooks Author can only be viewed on an iPad, the iPhone and iPod devices only have the capability to read EPUB and PDF books.

Getting ready

You need an iPad to test/preview your books on the iPad, so make sure you accessorize yourself with one.

How to do it...

To download iBooks Author, visit the App Store on your MacBook or iMac and search for `iBooks Author` to download and install it on your machine. It is a 270-MB download.

Exploring iBooks Author templates (Should know)

iBooks Author comes loaded with some default templates to get you started with your book-writing adventure; from simple textbook templates to cookbooks and photo books. When you load iBooks Author, the first window that loads prompts you to select a default template from the available library.

With Version 2.0 of iBooks Author, there is an option to select a **Portrait Only** mode that does not take the iPad orientation into consideration. This provides for better control of the layout.

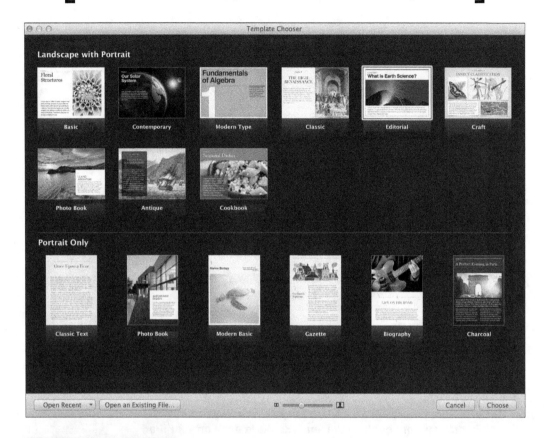

How to do it...

1. Open iBooks Author and select the **Basic** template from the **Landscape with Portrait** page. This is a sample book with the following pages:

    - **Book Title** page
    - **Table of Contents** page
    - **Glossary** page
    - **Intro Media** page—think of this as a splash screen for your book
    - A few pages of dummy content

2. We can customize this book by adding or replacing text, widgets, and other media, as can be seen in the following screenshot:

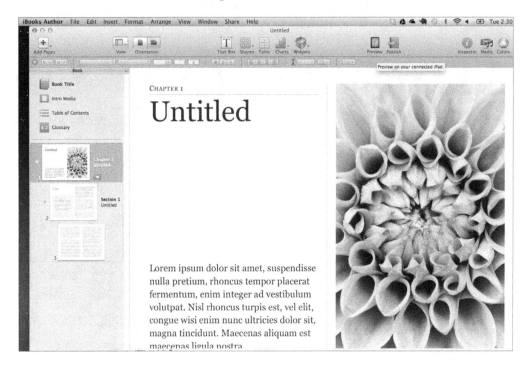

3. Similarly, to preview the book on your iPad, connect your iPad to your Mac and click on the **Preview** button to open your book on your iPad. Note that the iBooks app should be open on your iPad, otherwise you will see an error message such as the following:

To preview your book, make sure iBooks is open on your iPad

The other templates provide a similar interface to your book, just with a different look and feel and layout based on the template's theme. Besides the default templates available in iBooks Author, the Internet is full of templates for various types of books—some free templates, others need to be paid for.

A good set of free templates is **Templates for iBooks Author Free** available on the Mac App Store, `https://itunes.apple.com/us/app/templates-for-ibooks-author/id527161787?mt=12`, while there is a great number of paid templates, the most notable being **iBooks Author Templates** available at `http://www.ibooksauthortemplates.com/templates/all` and **Book Palette** from `http://www.jumsoft.com/book-palette/`.

Building a London travel guide with iBooks Author (Become an expert)

So far, we have seen how to add books and PDFs to iBooks, also, we played a bit with iBooks Author. Now let us create a full working book with iBooks Author titled London CityGuide. This will incorporate all the widgets and functions available within iBooks Author as well as a case study for layout/design.

The content will be travel-specific for London, sourced from www.WikiTravel.org, Wikipedia, and other open sources. Images will be from Creative Commons wherever possible, or free to use, depending on licenses from original owners.

The finished book is available for download via the iTunes store at https://itunes.apple.com/us/book/london/id593298852?ls=1.

How to do it...

1. Building the front page:

    i. Open iBooks Author and select the **Editorial** template. We will replace the placeholder image on the first page with an image of Tower Bridge from http://wikitravel.org/en/File:Tower_bridge_ London_Twilight_-_November_2006.jpg.

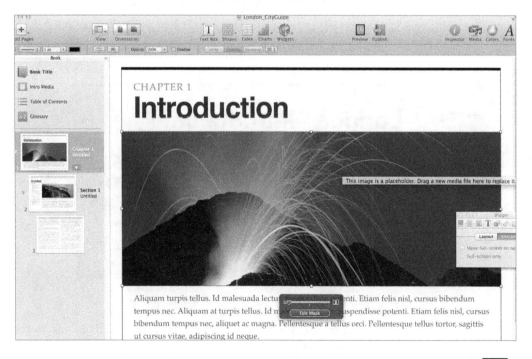

ii. Add the Tower Bridge image to your iPhoto library and then the image will be available for use within iBooks Author.

iii. Within iBooks Author, now you can drag this image to the placeholder image on the first page to make your page look like the following:

iv. Replace the dummy text on the introduction page with a generic description of London from WikiTravel. You may need to remove/edit some text to accommodate the spacing and layout; we have used the text "Noisy, vibrant and truly multicultural, London is a megalopolis of people, ideas and frenetic energy. The capital and largest city of both the United Kingdom and of England, it is also the largest city in Western Europe and the European Union. Situated on the River Thames, London remains an international capital of culture, music, education, fashion, politics, finance and trade."

v. Now for the book's cover page, let us use the Clock Tower photo from `http://wikitravel.org/en/File:Clock_Tower.jpg`. Now your book cover should look like the following; note that this is how the book will be displayed on the iBooks Bookshelf as well:

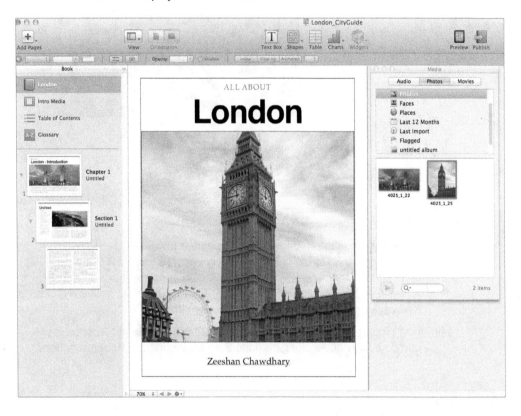

2. Building the History page:

i. The next page in our London CityGuide book will be a page that describes the history of the city of London. Click on page 2 of your book in iBooks; based on our template chosen earlier, page 2 of our book should look like the following screenshot:

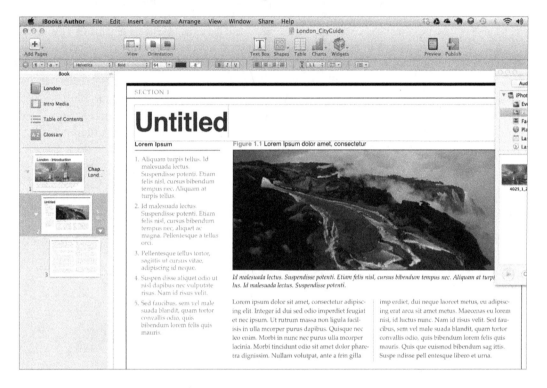

ii. We will now use information from Wikipedia (`http://en.wikipedia.org/wiki/London`) to build our History page. We copy the historical facts about London from Wikipedia, format it, and copy it to our page 2. As we keep adding content to our page, iBooks Author automatically adds new pages, depending upon the text.

iii. Don't forget to rename the title of page 2 from **Untitled** to `History`; you can do so by right-clicking on page 2 and selecting the **Rename** option.

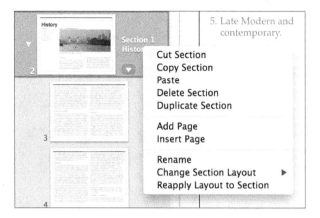

iv. After adding our history information from Wikipedia, our History page should now look like the following:

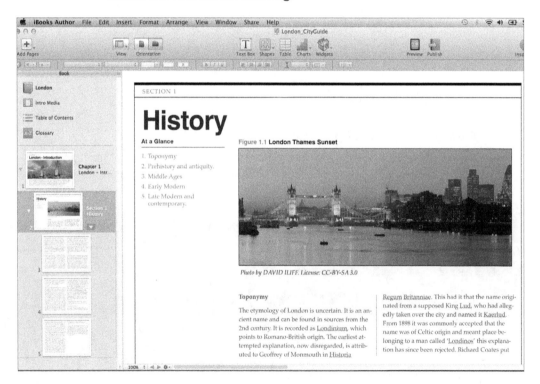

3. Building the Transportation page:

    i.   We will create another section in our book to accommodate the transportation information for London; we do so by copying the **Section 1** (History) page and renaming it to `Transportation`:

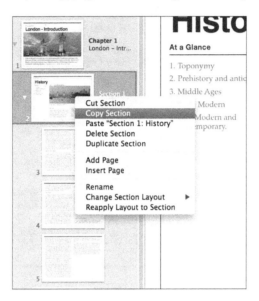

4. Previewing the books on your iPad:

    i.   Now would be a good time to have a quick look at the book and how it works on the iPad. The new iPad mini was used during the writing of this book. Now, we will move on to discussing how to preview books on your iPad (without submitting books to iBookstore).

    ii.   From within iBooks Author, click on the **Preview** button on the toolbar in the header.

 Make sure you have an iPad connected, as well as the iBooks app open.

    iii.   Here is how our London CityGuide book looks on an actual iPad, starting with the index page:

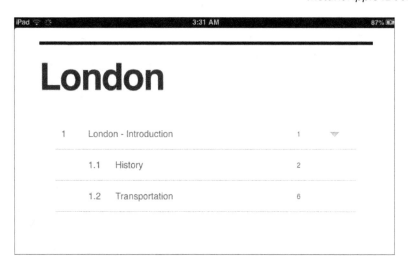

iv. Clicking on **Introduction** or swiping right-to-left (page-turn effect), shows us the Introduction page:

v. Similarly the **History** page (in landscape mode) looks stunning with the Thames river backdrop!

vi. While the **Transportation** page looks like the following:

5. Building the Culture page:

    i.   In the previous section, we added a new section to our book, using the copy-and-paste method. iBooks Author also provides another way to add pages, sections, or even chapters to our book via the **Add Pages** button in the header toolbar. We use the same method to add a new section to our book and name it `Culture`.

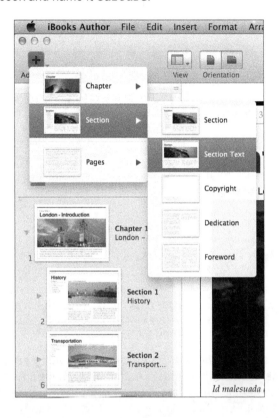

    ii.   We can also select the different layouts that we want for our section, as shown in the preceding image. We choose the **Section Text** layout for our Culture section. We then copy over the cultural information about London from Wikipedia onto our iBooks Author (after some formatting, by removing citations from the Wikipedia text). Note that on all the pages where we have used images to make our London CityGuide elegant, these images are sourced from Wikipedia and due attribution needs to be provided to the authors.

iii. Our **Culture** page now looks like the following:

Having added a few background and general information about London, let's move forward to adding new chapters for attractions, restaurants, and shopping.

6. Adding chapters for attractions and restaurants:

   i. We start by adding a new chapter using the **Add Pages** button from the header toolbar within iBooks Author and naming it as `Attractions`. The content for this chapter will be sourced from the WikiTravel page for London—`http://wikitravel.org/en/London#See`.

   ii. Similarly, we will add chapters for restaurants and add content from open source travel guide websites such as `www.Wikitravel.org` and `www.Wikipedia.org`. We will not go into the details of adding all the pages, since it is redundant, and by now you, the reader, should have a good idea of how things work with iBooks Author!

You can also choose to write you own content, maybe for your own hometown; get going around your town and get some pictures, and the rest is what we've already discussed.

iii. Here is how the **Attractions** page should look like; for the benefit of the readers, we are including the full source code and text for this book; the name of the file is `London_CityGuide.iba` and it is available for download via the book's page on `www.packtpub.com`.

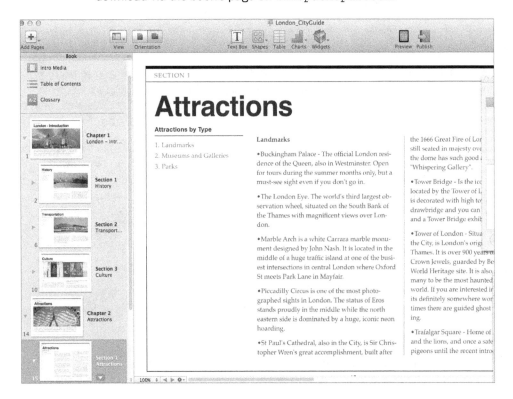

Adding HTML widgets and 3D models to your books (Become an expert)

There is more to an iBooks' book than text and images. With iBooks Author, you can add more interactivity to your books by adding HTML widgets and 3D models. Let's look at how iBooks Author helps us implement some of these exciting technologies in our books.

Getting ready

For our **Attractions** chapter we will add a few 3D models from Google Warehouse—`http://sketchup.google.com/3dwarehouse/`.

How to do it...

iBooks Author supports importing HTML5 widgets in the form of the `.wdgt` extension, which is basically a folder containing our HTML5 code, images, and an `Info.plist` file, which provides the iBooks app with information on how to run the HTML5 widget. We will create a simple Twitter widget that will pull information for the keyword "London" from Twitter.

1. Create a folder and name it `twitter-widget-ibooks`, and within the folder create an `index.html` file using your favorite text editor. Using a simple Twitter Mashup from `http://www.designchemical.com/blog/index.php/jquery/jquery-tutorial-create-a-jquery-twitter-feed-plugin/`, we modify the code to search for the keyword "London".

2. Here is how the HTML page should look now:

3. Rename the `twitter-widget-ibooks folder` to `twitter-widget-ibooks.wdgt`; the folder icon should now look like a widget icon.

4. Once the widget is ready, open iBooks Author and reload our London CityGuide book. Within the **History** section of the first chapter, insert an HTML widget using the **Widgets** button the toolbar, as shown in the following screenshot:

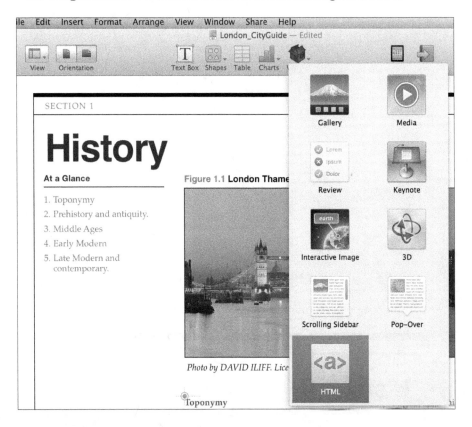

5. Drag the HTML widget under the **At a Glance** section, and keeping the HTML widget selected, under the **Interaction** tab in **Inspector**, select the `twitter-widget-ibooks.wdgt` widget we created before:

6. Previewing the book on your iPad shows the following results:

7. To see the real-time tweets for London, click the Twitter icon, and you should see an overlay with real-time tweets for London. Clicking on the **X** icon on the overlay will bring you back to the book's page.

8. Similarly, iBooks Author also supports importing 3D models as an interactive content within our books. Download a COLLADA (`.dae` file) model from `http://sketchup.google.com/3dwarehouse/details?mid=e47ab8e194c03e5d5e73daf3c0b064fa`.

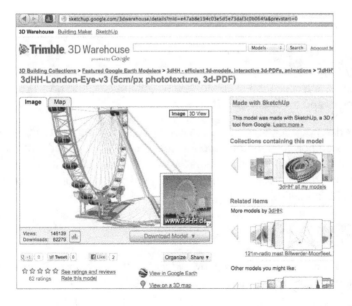

9. Extract the 3D model and import the same within our **Attractions** chapter, as shown in the following screenshot:

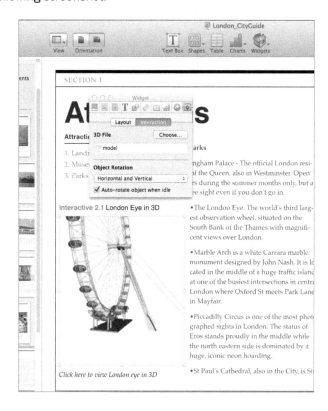

10. Preview the book on your iPad to see the 3D model in action!

How it works...

The HTML5 widget is a collection of HTML, JavaScript, images, and an `Info.plist` file that notifies the iBooks app to render an HTML code.

Apple has added support for 3D objects in a completed book with up to 50,000 moderately-textured polygons for the second-generation iPad and iPads with a Retina display; for the first-gen iPad, this number is 20,000. The format supported right now is COLLADA—an interchangeable file format for 3D applications supported by most companies and 3D modeling software.

There's more...

Apple has put a good overview on how HTML widgets can be compiled, and specifications for the can be found at `http://support.apple.com/kb/HT5068`.

Troubleshooting common errors (Must know)

Question: I cannot preview my book on my iPad from iBooks Author.

Answer: Make sure the iBooks app on your iPad is open and you have connected your iPad to your MacBook or iMac.

Question: I cannot download some books from iBookstore.

Answer: The iBookstore collection varies from country to country; some books may not be available in all countries.

Question: Does iBooks Author support custom fonts?

Answer: Yes, iBooks Author supports custom fonts; only true type fonts (`.ttf`) and open type fonts (`.otf`) are supported for now.

Question: Can I sell my books on iBookstore?

Answer: Yes, you can distribute your books for free or can allow paid books to be downloaded from the iBookstore similar to paid apps, with the 70-30 distribution model.

Question: Can I export my book created with iBooks Author in other formats?

Answer: Yes, iBooks Author supports exporting the book in PDF and plain text.

Question: My 3D model does not load quickly in my book.

Answer: This may depend on the number of polygons in your 3D models, for large models, try to reduce the polygon count for faster loads.

Thank you for buying
Instant Apple iBooks How-to

About Packt Publishing

Packt, pronounced 'packed', published its first book "*Mastering phpMyAdmin for Effective MySQL Management*" in April 2004 and subsequently continued to specialize in publishing highly focused books on specific technologies and solutions.

Our books and publications share the experiences of your fellow IT professionals in adapting and customizing today's systems, applications, and frameworks. Our solution based books give you the knowledge and power to customize the software and technologies you're using to get the job done. Packt books are more specific and less general than the IT books you have seen in the past. Our unique business model allows us to bring you more focused information, giving you more of what you need to know, and less of what you don't.

Packt is a modern, yet unique publishing company, which focuses on producing quality, cutting-edge books for communities of developers, administrators, and newbies alike. For more information, please visit our website: www.packtpub.com.

Writing for Packt

We welcome all inquiries from people who are interested in authoring. Book proposals should be sent to author@packtpub.com. If your book idea is still at an early stage and you would like to discuss it first before writing a formal book proposal, contact us; one of our commissioning editors will get in touch with you.

We're not just looking for published authors; if you have strong technical skills but no writing experience, our experienced editors can help you develop a writing career, or simply get some additional reward for your expertise.

iOS 5 Essentials

ISBN: 978-1-84969-226-7   Paperback: 252 pages

Harness iOS 5's new powerful features to create stunning applications

1. Integrate iCloud, Twitter, and AirPlay into your applications.

2. Lots of step-by-step examples, images, and diagrams to get you up to speed in no time with helpful hints along the way.

3. Each chapter explains iOS 5's new features indepth, whilst providing you with enough practical examples to help incorporate these features in your apps.

iAd Production Beginner's Guide

ISBN: 978-1-84969-132-1   Paperback: 240 pages

Create motion-rich, beautiful iAd adverts for iOS devices and incorporate techniques to help boost revenue and brand awareness

1. Create interactive iAd mobile adverts that appear in applications downloaded from the App Store.

2. Learn to use the drag-and-drop visual tool, iAd Producer, to create ads without any experience with the underlying technologies.

3. Reach an audience that downloads over 200 apps per second and leave a lasting, memorable image of your brand with rich immersive ads.

Please check **www.packtpub.com** for information on our titles

Instant New iPad Features in iOS 6 How-to [Instant]

ISBN: 978-1-78216-046-5   Paperback: 74 pages

Learn to use Mail, iCloud, Photo Stream, iPhoto, iWorks, iTunes, iMovie, and Garageband through easy-to-follow recipes

1. Learn something new in an Instant! A short, fast, focused guide delivering immediate results.

2. Set up Mail using multiple accounts and a VIP Inbox.

3. Enable iCloud for synchronous use with other Apple devices and programs.

4. Understand Photo Stream and its key features.

iWork for Mac OS X Cookbook

ISBN: 978-1-84969-310-3   Paperback: 324 pages

Over 50 recipes which go beyong the manuals and explore the incredible potential of iWork to do the job of a full creative suite

1. Explodes the widely held view that iWork is simply Apple's version of MS Office by revealing the amazing creative power of this office suite.

2. Use iWork to create high quality documents for professional printing or internet use.

3. Written for both the new and experienced iWork users, this book is a step-by-step guide to creating dazzling graphics, unique clip art, logos, and sophisticated designs to rival top-end professional programs.

Please check **www.packtpub.com** for information on our titles